EXQUISITE BLOODY, BEATING HEART

Courtney LeBlanc

Riot in Your Throat
publishing fierce, feminist poetry

Copyright © Courtney LeBlanc 2021

No part of this book may be used or performed without written consent from the author, if living, except for critical articles or reviews.

LeBlanc, Courtney.
1st edition.
ISBN: 978-1-7361386-1-8

Cover Art: Victoria Olt
Cover Design: Kirsten Birst
Book Design: Shanna Compton
Author Photo: Joey Clinton

Riot in Your Throat
Arlington, VA
www.riotinyourthroat.com

To anyone who ever wondered if I'm writing about you. I am.

CONTENTS

THIS IS WHAT WOMEN DO

13 Autobiography of Eve
14 We Carry
15 Alternative Names for Woman
16 We're Told to Smile
17 Her Becoming
18 To the Man Who Shouted "What does your pussy taste like?!" As I Ran By
19 Gasoline
20 My Current Favorite Is Called Blackmail
21 Or Worse
22 First Date
23 Promotion
24 Poem Where I Mix-Up Fairy Tales
25 On the Way to a Cocktail Reception for Work
26 How Empty Those Roads Were
27 Tradition
28 First Punch
29 Butcher

ALL I'VE SWALLOWED

33 A Girl Becomes a Woman
34 Original Sin
35 Other Than Desire
36 Hunger Lectures Me
37 This Body

38 Skinny Dreams
39 Love Poem to My Scoliosis
41 Did Not
42 Sixteen
43 Construction
44 Ode to My Vibrator
45 Post-Sex Snack
46 Imagine What My Body Will Sound Like
47 Morning Tableau

MOUTHING YOUR MEMORY

51 A Choose Your Own Path Poem
52 Collapse
54 Remember the Ocean
55 Postcards Never Written
56 Starved
57 Paris Imploding
58 I'm Always the Refrain in Your Songs
59 Starfish
61 Blood Orange
62 Surrender
63 Goat of My Heart
64 Pearl
65 Self-Portrait as a Form Rejection Letter
67 How to Run

EXQUISITE BLOODY, BEATING HEART

71 Constellation
72 The Weight of Water

73	Pompeii
74	I Don't Write Many Nice Poems About Him
75	Jolene
77	To My Ex Who Asked if Every Poem Was About Him
78	Poem in Which Nothing Bad Ever Happens to Me
81	The First Post-Marriage Fuck
83	The Craigslist Missed Connection I Didn't Write
84	Before the Occasion of Your Death
86	Honest Answer
87	The Pleasure of Hating
89	Garden
90	Elegy For My Still-Living Husband
91	Love Is a Lesion on Your Brain
93	Eventually Evolution
95	Thanks
96	Acknowledgments & Notes
100	About the Author
101	About the Press

THIS IS WHAT WOMEN DO

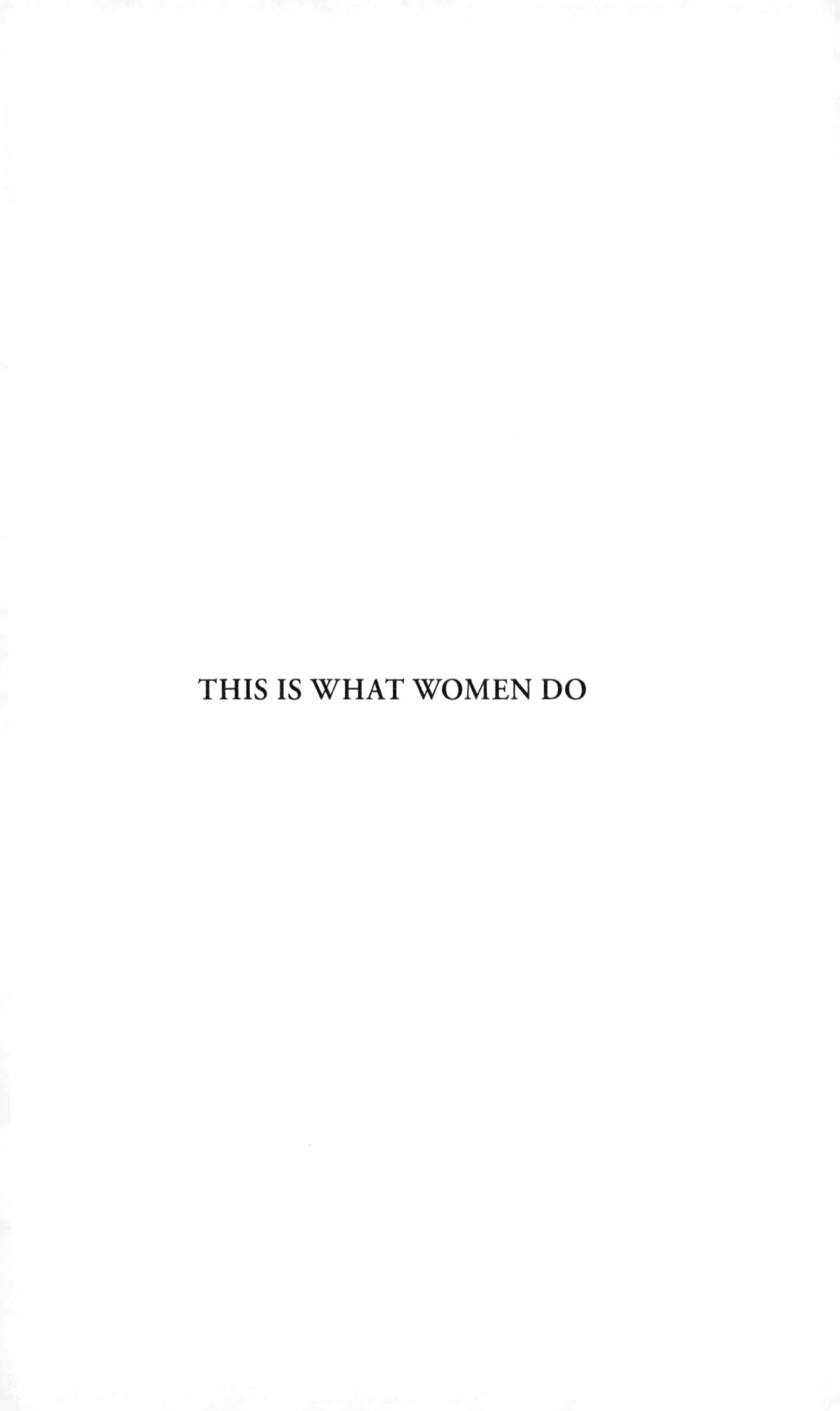

AUTOBIOGRAPHY OF EVE

Wearing nothing but snakeskin boots
I left, walked away
from the man I called *husband*,
the booming voice I called *father*.
I walked till the blisters formed
and then popped, oozed pus into my boots.
His first wife, Lilith, had come this way
and I needed to find her. She'd been right
about it all—the blame, the bullshit,
the blasphemy. Now that the sticky juice
of knowledge ran freely down my chin
I wanted to hold her hand and discover
all I didn't yet know.

WE CARRY

We carry our lipstick which we always forget
to reapply after dinner. We carry our keys,
clutched between fingers like brass knuckles.
We carry our empty wallets and the tears from the angry
phone call with our mothers. We carry condoms
and when those break we carry Plan B. We carry
our pride and our shame and the diet pills that made our hearts
race but *damn girl*, look at these thin thighs. We carry the last
Post-it note he left on the mirror and we carry the receipt
from therapy. We carry the eyeliner smudged from last night's
drinks and ibuprofen for today's hangover. We carry the crystals
to ward off evil, to bring luck, to add heft and make our bag
a weapon. We carry the fortune we got on that good date
with the blond who seemingly lost our number the next morning.
We carry the crumpled business card from the guy who bought
drinks even after we said *no thanks*. We carry our best friend
when she loses the baby. We carry the cost of our birth control
when our employer's insurance refuses to pay. We carry the rent
check, the student loan debt, the grocery bill. We carry our hearts
when they got too muddied on our sleeves. We carry flip-flops
to slip onto our feet after a long day in heels. We carry cardigans
after being told our shoulders were too provocative. We carry
the fingerprint bruises and the *I ran into the door* excuses. We
carry it all, the heavy world digging into our shoulders
and slumping our backs.

ALTERNATIVE NAMES FOR WOMAN
after Danez Smith

79 cents to a dollar
dramatic
bossy
bitch
stepping stone
support position
secretary—no, administrative assistant
old hag
witch
kitchen dweller
dinner maker
baby maker
glass ceiling breaker
Senator, Justice, Secretary of State
President
President
President

WE'RE TOLD TO SMILE

because this is what women do: we smile
through the insults, through the *well I thought
you wouldn't mind*, through the paraphrasing
of what we just said because clearly it makes
more sense coming from a deeper voice.
We smile through the missed promotions
and the limited funding. We smile through
being called Mrs. when Dr. is correct.
We smile through getting called *honey*
and *sugar* and *baby*. We smile through
it was only a joke and *don't take everything
so seriously*. We smile through judgments
on our breasts, our hips, our legs, our asses.
We smile through the *accidental* touches,
the *well-intended* suggestions, the *good-
natured* flirting. We smile through your leg
pressing against ours on trains, on buses.
We smile because we're *making a big deal
out of nothing*. We smile because if we didn't
our teeth might get knocked out, our throats
crushed—a reminder of all we have
to smile about.

HER BECOMING

Needed no snake. Grew the fruit myself. Was the vine
and the rain and the light. Was the dirt. The hand
reaching out, fingering the sweet swell, the sharp
crunch of my teeth sinking into skin, the crisp
taste in my mouth.

Needed no forked tongue tickling my ear, cooed
the words to myself, a lullaby, a love song.
I wanted, I took.

When only the poison seeds clinging to the core remained
I tossed it aside, kicked dirt over it. The seeds might grow
into a new tree, might feed another girl's hunger,
be the key to her own opening, her becoming.

TO THE MAN WHO SHOUTED "WHAT DOES YOUR PUSSY TASTE LIKE?!" AS I RAN BY

It tastes briny,
like the ocean.
It surges, waves pounding
the surf, punishing
the sand simply for always
being there, for always
being present, for never
leaving well enough alone.

I keep running,
ready to drown him
in a sea of my pounding
feet.

GASOLINE

The man who grabbed / my ass on the train / gasoline / the man could have passed / as Santa / calling me *honey* / gasoline / the man who sank / his fingers / inside of me / before I could push / him away / gasoline / the man who tried to fuck me / with an empty beer bottle / when I was seventeen / gasoline / the man / who called / me *sweetheart* / in a meeting / gasoline / I'm peeling / back my skin / revealing / the flint of a match / crawling through my blood / my bones / I'm ready / to burn / this fucking frat party / this America to the ground.

MY CURRENT FAVORITE IS CALLED BLACKMAIL

I've started wearing dark lipstick, stand
in front of the mirror drawing
the bow of my upper lip, making it fuller
than it really is, a magic trick only women
are taught. The first day I wear it a woman
I don't know tells I'm brave for wearing
such a dark color into the office. A man tells
me he likes the color. Before I can say
thank you he continues: *It would look good
ringing my cock*. I peel back my lips, bared
teeth bright white against my dark mouth.

OR WORSE

She shakes, her muscled body reduced
to quivering fear—the bus that rumbled
by, terrifying her, taking her to a place
I can't reach. I try anyway, wrap my arms
around her quaking body, my voice soothing
even as her ears flatten and she strains
against me. When she calms enough to walk
we turn quickly toward home, no other
destination considered. A neighbor, well-
meaning no doubt, tells me I need
to be in charge, that my dog could bite
me—or worse—if I let her have control.
I am usually kind, try to be pleasant,
but like my dog, I too, am triggered and tired
of old, white men telling me what to do.
I just stare at him, ready to bite—or worse.

FIRST DATE

Women can't drive my car, he said, adjusting his mirrored sunglasses. *Because it's stick?* I asked. *Because they don't know how to drive fast,* he said. My mind flashed a warning like flares after an accident. In his lenses I saw my reflection and the two roads before me—the girl who could giggle and ignore it or the girl who refused to be his assumption. I held my hand out. *Give me the keys.* I gunned the engine, left tire tracks on the pavement, looping like an autograph. He watched the needle of the speedometer pulse—a thin red knife, thin as the stretched smile he'd given me when we first met. I laughed and pushed harder, foot pressing down on pedal, pressing down on the bullshit line he'd given me, pressing down on every bullshit line every man had ever given me. I hit triple digits—I'd never driven this fast before. I pulled back into his lot and popped the brake, returning him to the place he'd crawled out from under. I tossed him the keys and walked away, left him standing in the parking lot. I reapplied my lipstick, didn't bother to watch him grow small in the rearview mirror as I drove away.

PROMOTION

I sit with hands wrapped
around the steaming mug.
My new office is freezing,
my desk just below
the vents that blow cold
air regardless of the outside
temperature. I sit and sip
hot water—not tea or coffee,
just water. Just the mug to warm
my hands and the liquid
to warm my throat.

Only men have inhabited
this space and I knew
it would be cold but
the requirement of layers
and a lined bra seemed
a worthy trade-off
for authority and power.

I celebrate
by ordering business cards
with my new title
printed on them.
Tomorrow I'll wear
an unlined bra.
I'll let my erect
nipples walk into the room
before me—guns blazing.

POEM WHERE I MIX-UP FAIRY TALES

Sometimes the wolf shows up in a suit,
hair neat and tie perfect, teeth tucked
into his mouth to mimic a sly smile.
Sometimes he's a friend, sometimes
a stranger, sometimes a lover.
Sometimes I crave the beast's
hands on my skin, sometimes I want
his bite, sometimes I don't want
to be rescued. I wish this sleep could
last forever, my still body tended
by the forest and the animals, hidden
from the prince's kiss—why wake
up in a world that constantly kicks
and takes away my rights? I'll take
the beast to get his library, I'll take
the spindle to finally catch up
on my sleep, I'll take the wolf
to avoid future errands. And
that house of sugar? I'll lick
every windowpane and wait
for the witch. She won't push me
into the fire; instead we'll sit
around it, spiked drinks in hand,
munching on cookies, toasting
our luck at finding one another.

ON THE WAY TO A COCKTAIL RECEPTION FOR WORK

This life isn't / what I expected / how am I sitting in these meetings / stiletto heels / and business cards with / my name / boss lady / money maker / game changer / sometimes / I still cry / in the bathroom / still fake it / still worry / this isn't my / life / I ~~died~~ dyed / my hair / purple / pull it back / top knot / top bitch / still hustling / still writing / still wondering / what I'm doing.

HOW EMPTY THOSE ROADS WERE

The wood and glass case in the corner
of the family room, the key conspicuously
on top of it: I grew up around guns. The gun
rack in the rear window of the truck;
occasionally, a barrel down, butt up between
the front seat of the old farm truck, the one
we never drove off our dirt roads. I remember
my father aiming at the coyote that stalked
our fields, my fingers pressed into my ears
to muffle the crack of the shot, how I still
heard it and the animal's near-simultaneous
yelp as the hot metal bit into its flesh. The vast
lands of our fields echoed the vast lands
of our state—how empty those roads were
as I drove my friend 8 hours to the state's only
clinic. I held her hand when we walked up, my eyes
on the trucks that lined the street, the gun racks filled
with the 2nd amendment that had no desire to protect us.

TRADITION

I went with my mother, honored tradition
for her sake. I pulled a dress from the rack—
glossy white but with black lace dancing
up the bodice. I loved the contrast, the twist.
I brought my fiancé with us, watched the look
of horror on the saleswoman's face. I'm not
superstitious, didn't care what of mine he saw
before the wedding. Ultimately, it didn't matter—
the dress was discontinued, a basic white chosen
in its place. For the ceremony I chose nothing
blue, nothing old. Maybe if I'd followed
tradition my marriage would have survived.
But I doubt a scrap of blue could have saved
us. When he remarried, his new bride obeyed
all the rules.

FIRST PUNCH

Before you label me slut / bitch / cunt know this: he told me
he was single and she should have used his body
for a punching bag the way he'd used mine
for pleasure. I didn't see it coming, didn't see her
fist flying toward my face like a stone. I was lucky
I was fast, turning enough for her fist to glance off
my cheekbone instead of landing square. And then
I was out the door, feet propelling me down
the dark street. He caught up to me several blocks later, offered
to drive me home. When he rolled to a stop in front of my house
he asked to come in, he wanted inside me again. My head
ached, my cheek swollen but not yet turning the pale green
of a sunset. I reared back and threw my first punch, landed my fist
square to his nose, left him bleeding in the front seat.

BUTCHER

I told him before our clothes fell
to the floor. He insisted he didn't
care. Later, after we showered,
he tells me he hates blood,
how disgusting it is, how I've ruined
his sheets. I tell him of the butchering
season each year, my father slicing
the cow's throat, its scream
drowning in the warm blood
that gushed over my father's hand
as he held the head back.
I tell him of the hide peeled back,
the meat sliced from bone. I detail
the organs I cut into chunks
for the dog—the liver, the kidneys—
thick with blood. I don't stop
until the blood drains from
his face and he retches, hand over mouth
as he runs to the bathroom. When I leave
I don't look back.

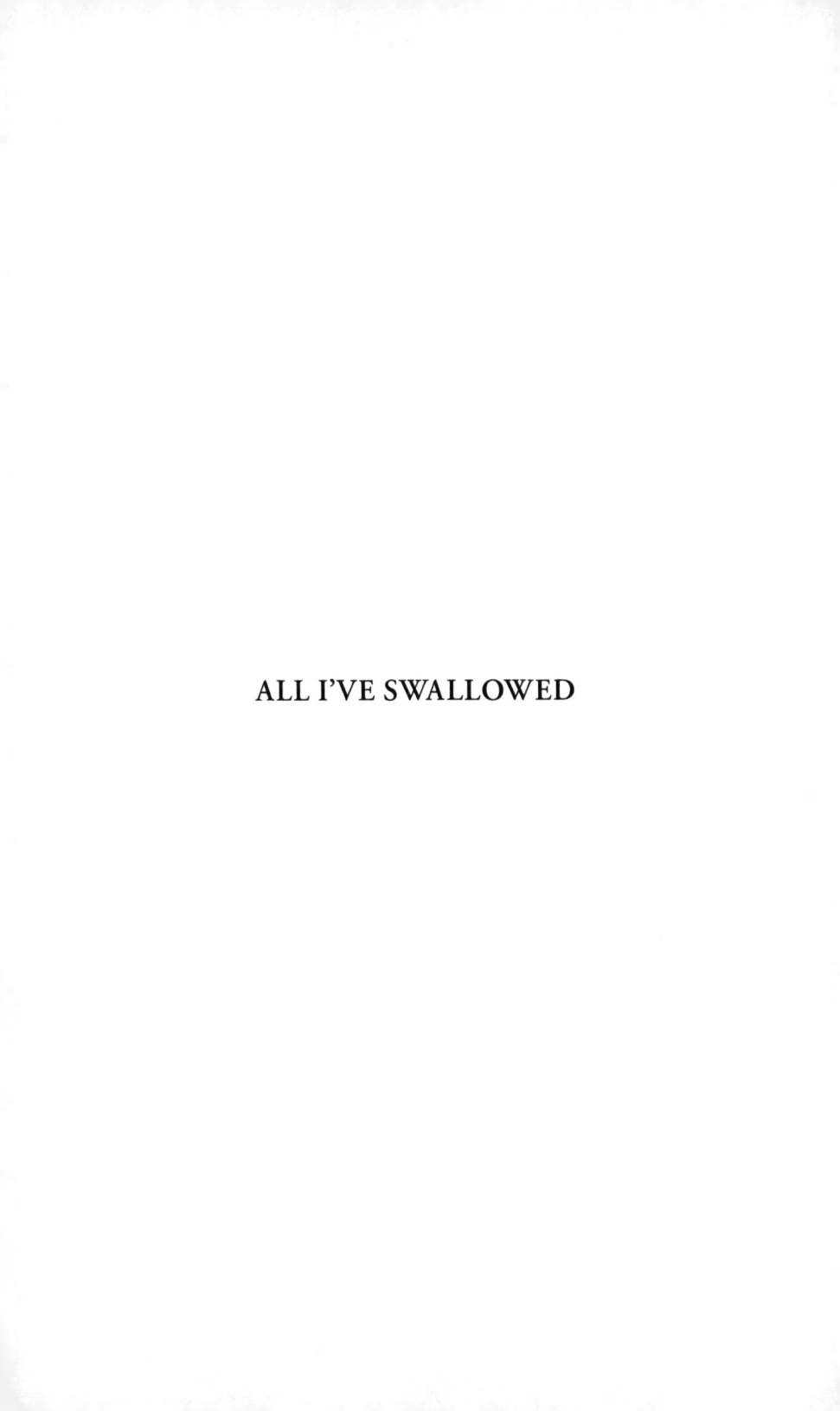

ALL I'VE SWALLOWED

A GIRL BECOMES A WOMAN

> *a child learns the world by putting it in her mouth,*
> *a girl becomes a woman and a woman, earth.*
> —Ilya Kaminsky, "Firing Squad"

I think of everything I've put
into my mouth, all I've swallowed.
At first, words: *no, stop, I've changed*
my mind. Then my hands, my feet,
my ability to fight, to run away.
I swallowed my voice, grew smaller, shrank
till my hip bones jutted like handlebars—till
I could be steered in the desired direction.
I chewed off my skin, removed the dark ink
that bloomed on my arms, my back. Revealed
the unblemished baby-pink. I keep swallowing
till there's nothing left, till I disappear into the dirt,
the earth finally swallowing me.

ORIGINAL SIN

When I was seventeen my daily
lunch was an apple and two
rice cakes. Every day I peeled
the sticker from the apple's skin,
stuck it to the inside
of my locker door, insisted
I'd had a big breakfast and didn't
waver from this routine
for an entire year.
I never once thought about
Eve or her apple or the original
sin, how hunger and desire
rumbled deep within her.
I thought only of my own naked
body, my own soft thighs, the gap
between them widening.

OTHER THAN DESIRE

I stare at the cookies, brownies, cakes. I don't even like
sweets but any bakery tempts me with their confections.
I don't eat them, can't let my body be filled with
anything other than desire. I eye-fuck the cupcakes,
press a hand to my yawning belly, find my hipbones,
hold onto them like handlebars. I'll pedal this slender
body straight into a sugar factory, make snow angels
in the crystals, snort powdered sugar, rub it into my
gums. It leaves me shaky and tingly till I purge, my
eyes watery, cheeks flushed, throat burning from
the acid brought up. I check my reflection in the mirror,
suck in my stomach, wonder if I'll ever let anything stay.

HUNGER LECTURES ME

People are starving and there you sit with $200 in weekly
groceries in your organized pantry, the labeled containers
of flour and sugar and rice, your fridge with soy milk
and eggs and two steaks, thick with blood, the produce
basket overflowing with mangoes and clementines
and tomatoes, and you're entering every calorie
into your phone, making sure you stay under the allotted
daily intake. You were poor farmers growing up but there
were always the vegetables you grew, the beef you raised—
your plates were never empty, even if they lacked variety.
Your mother was a boring cook but there was always enough
for all four kids. By the time you were sixteen you decided
the small curve of your belly was too much, your thighs too
soft. Puberty added pounds so you decided they needed
to go, decided 99 pounds was acceptable. You were running
75 miles a week, the sweet-coated laxatives you ate like
the world's worst candy, belly cramping in the middle of the night
as you shit out every morsel you swallowed that day. How you still
flirt with this in the recording every calorie consumed, live by
the mantra *ya gotta burn it to earn it*. Oh shut up you skinny bitch
and eat that brownie, it's gooey and warm and slightly undercooked,
exactly how you like it.

THIS BODY

This body is a war
zone. This body is a grenade
tossed inside the Senate
building. This body is pulled
apart—a mouth taken
as souvenir, a hand pinned
to a wall, splayed beneath glass
like a butterfly, a vagina
in a pocket for ease
of use. This body is a machine,
programmed to make breakfast
and babies. This body is a natural
disaster, raging tsunamis
and blazing forest fires. This body
is a toy, played with
then discarded. This body
is a weapon, razor sharp
and ready to cut.
This body is.

SKINNY DREAMS

The way my clavicles arch out, create a hollow
at the base of my neck. How I track calories,
my phone in my fist after every meal, measuring
every morsel that slides down my throat. The scale
that sits quietly in the corner, pulled out each
morning at the same time, my naked skin glowing
in the dark, predicting the rest of my day.
The smell of brownies baking, rich chocolate
filling the house. I eat one, take the rest
into the office—how I'm loved by my coworkers.
The lines of definition in my biceps, the curve
of my calves, the hollow dip where I once
had a belly. My hip bones jutting out beneath
my skin, perfect hooks for hands or underwear.
And how my belly growls late at night, a lullaby.

LOVE POEM TO MY SCOLIOSIS

O crooked spine, o curved
skeletal frame, you grew
an extra vertebra and curved
to the left, refused gravity's
downward pull. You send me
to the ER annually, seeking
syringes filled with drugs
to stop your frantic spasms,
the grip you know only
to tighten. Gave yourself
a pretty name—scoliosis—
and caused me to cry when you
were discovered at sixteen:
too late to correct, too late
to stop your sideways march.
O compressed spinal cord,
you send messages to my
fingertips—electric and
tingling. You hold one hip
higher, pull the same shoulder
down, attempting a tango
between body parts, the muscles
in the middle stuck in a crushing
embrace. The knobs of my
spine turned to the left,
a lopsided ladder for my lover's
hands to climb. And how you
bend out half my ribs while

crushing the other side, the wide
breath I pull in to fill you, to ease
me through the stiffness and ache
you bring me most days. O twisted
bones, o curved frame—I call you
beloved, I call you beautiful.
I call you mine.

DID NOT

I did not toss the empty beer bottle out
the window, did not watch it disappear
in the tall grass. Did not turn my head to hide
the blush when he said, *If it didn't break
that means you're still a virgin*. Did not
acknowledge the warmth spreading
through my center. Later, when I took
him in my mouth I did not resist the pressure
of his hand on the back of my head, did not
know that pushing back was an option.
But also, I did not "finish", did not know
there was a finale I was withholding
from him. I did not get the *blue balls*
joke he dropped in front of his friends
that summer. He did not kiss anything
other than my lips, no matter how many
backseats we climbed into. He did not ask
if I enjoyed it when his hand crept down
my pants as we drove back country roads.
And while I did not know it at the time,
for I did not have a map to the body
I was newly exploring, I did not allow him
the full pleasure of me, not once.

SIXTEEN

I planted hands on his broad chest and pushed
but he held firm, his weight a bulldozer
against me. He was older and experienced
and fascinated with my narrow waist,
the way his hands could circle almost
all the way around. The next day he left
for his out-of-state college, start of his junior
year. I returned to my parents' house,
to cross-country practice. Ran ten miles a day.
Waited for his phone call. Every night I slept
in the fleece sweatshirt he'd left, his college
mascot embroidered on the chest, several sizes
too big for me. When he asked for it back I returned
it to his parents, his mother gentle when she took
it from my hand, as if she knew all the parts of me
her son had broken.

CONSTRUCTION

He built houses, moved from town
to town with his company. I met him
the summer I was nineteen—wild
and lean-limbed and tan. One night
we went to his job site, walked into
the skeleton of a house, climbed
the railless stairs to the second floor.
The roof would go on next week
but that night the stars were ours.
He spread the blanket and we lay
down, eyes cast upward till I rolled
on top of him. Every time he came
to town that summer he called me
and we fucked in unfinished houses,
christening each one before the owners
could. When the days grew shorter,
the nights cooler, he headed south, chasing
the work. Every time I drove past new
housing developments I thought of him,
his mouth on my skin, the sky reckless
and bright around us.

ODE TO MY VIBRATOR

Thank you, you beautiful pink bullet, you humming toy of joy. Thank you for the small satin bag you came in, your desire to travel easily, your discretion. Thank you for your multiple settings, for your push-button ease. Thank you for convenient USB charging capability. Thank you for always finding my spot, for not demanding foreplay or cuddling after, for not being upset if I don't moan or call out your name. Thank you for letting me fall asleep immediately and for not hogging the best pillow. Thank you for your endless give, for never making me return the favor. Thank you for my satisfaction being your only job.

POST-SEX SNACK

I drag the knife across the skin
of a mango, travel the circumference
of its red-green shell, a bead
of juice seeping out at the seam.
Dig my fingers into the flesh,
break the fruit apart into uneven
halves. I hand one to you, lift the other
to my mouth and bite the flesh,
juice running down my chin,
streaking my neck. You eat until
only the deflated skin remains.
I gnaw at the pit, mouth it
smooth. You dip your head, lick
rivers of juice from my breasts.

IMAGINE WHAT MY BODY WILL SOUND LIKE

The dog is mouthing the ball, lying
with his back toward us, protecting
his toy from thieving hands. My husband
says, *that sounds like the worst oral sex*,
and we all groan and inevitably focus
on the noise. I think of porn, how
the women are always smooth-skinned
and hair-free, mouths wide and moaning
in faked pleasure. Women making noise
seems to be expected, demanded.
Once I was with a man who made no noise
when he fucked me, not a single slipped
whimper. When I'm alone, buzzing toy
in hand, I make no noise, I don't need
to impress or indulge myself. And when I cum—
eyes closed, entire body clenched in a tsunami
of pleasure—I don't think of the noises
I could make, the quaking inside me
an ocean roaring in my ears.

MORNING TABLEAU

I stand naked in my kitchen, lights off and blinds open
waiting for my coffee to brew. I do this every morning,
navigate my home in the dark because I refuse
to put on clothes after I shower. I keep
the lights off because I never remember to close
the blinds and my neighbors would have a perfect
view of my breasts, nipples hard in the cool morning
air, the heat turned down because I like it cold when I sleep.
When the machine stops gurgling, I pick up my coffee mug,
feel the hot liquid travel down my throat, my skin flush
from the sudden warmth. Sometimes I'm tempted
to turn the light on, to throw myself
into bright relief like a deer in headlights—to capture
the beauty and starkness of the moment: my pale skin
bright, my coffee mug steaming, my surprised eyes
and smiling mouth—the perfect morning tableau.

MOUTHING YOUR MEMORY

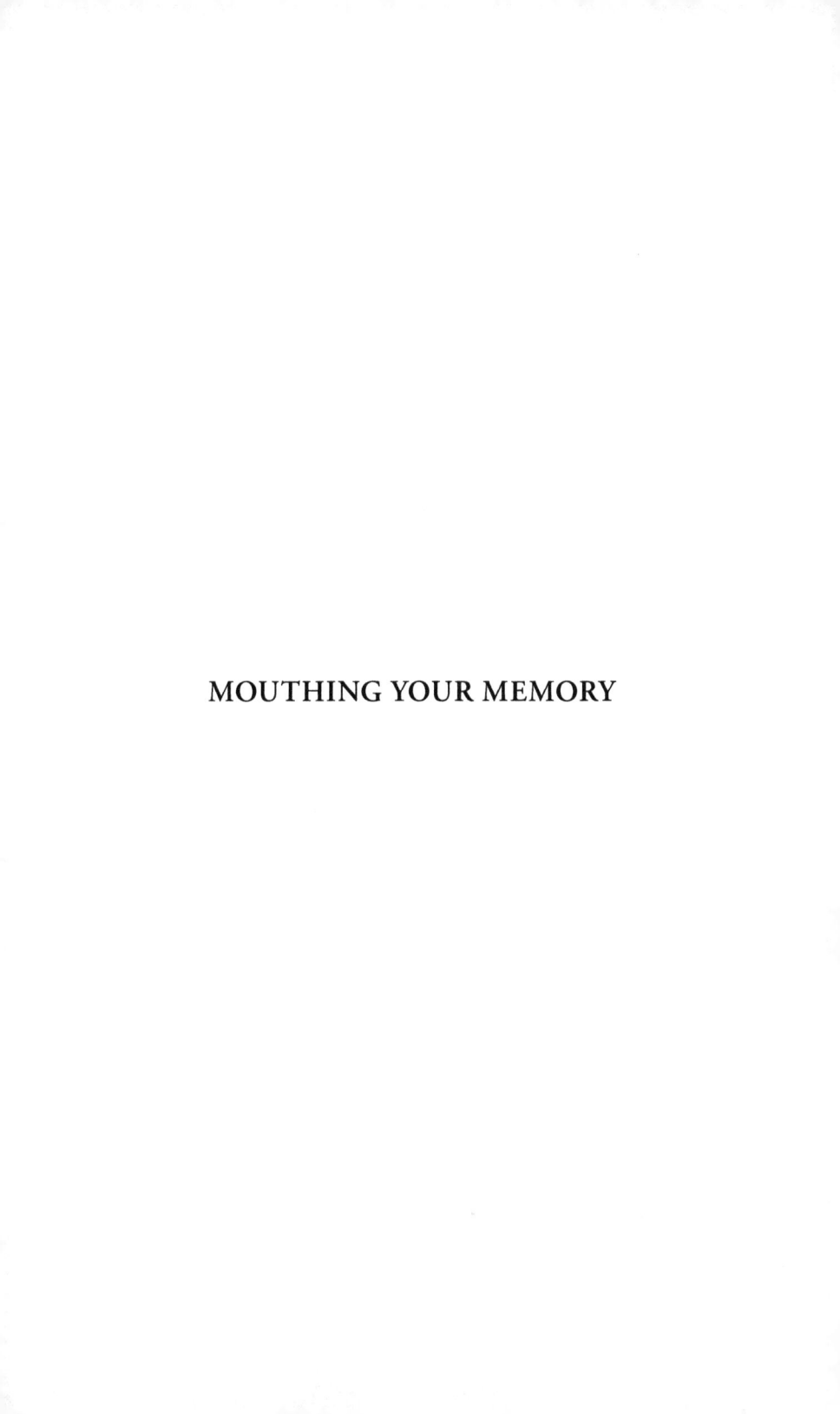

A CHOOSE YOUR OWN PATH POEM

I [forgive/hate] myself for the first time
we touched. How I opened for you
like a flower, bloomed in the dark
hours of the night.

I [hate/forgive] myself that I saw
you again and again, every night
for a week. Pulled your lips
to mine to ease the gnawing
hunger that chewed at my heart.

I [forgive/hate] myself for wanting
your mouth on me, for craving
salt and your skin.

I [hate/forgive] myself for the lies
I told—to others, to myself,
to the stranger on the beach
who asked how long we'd
been together.

I [forgive/hate] myself for the secrets
that grew like a monster
under the bed, ready to pounce
and devour me at any moment.

I [hate/forgive] myself.

COLLAPSE

We arrived in sunlight and departed in sunlight,
the summer sky turning pink, turning blue, purple,
black. Summer of meteors and shooting stars.
A collision of stars can cause a black hole—they sink
to the center of the galaxy: a black hole is anything but
empty space.

We waited till nightfall to touch, the daylight hours
spooled out before us, waited for the stars to blink
into existence. The heat of the day still radiated off
our bodies, the thin crust of sweat still clung to our skin.
Lying on our backs, we searched the sky for the shooting stars,
I longed for the tenor of your voice to break the night's
silence. When Orion appeared, I moved my mouth
to yours, fell into you.

The pressure of one body against another: summer,
waxed and honeyed. Seeking out constellations
and your skin. Thinking about the mystery of black
holes, how you too are beautiful and deadly
and unknown till now.

The bonfire we built dies, the smoke reminding
me of that last, long summer: the kittens born
too early, my sister and I still running like children
through the tall grass, even as my breasts began
to bud. The sky was drinkable, dazzling, white
and we didn't know that night our house would

burn. If we had would we remember the sun
muted? Would we notice the lilacs, still blooming
behind the house, the air drunk with their scent?

My sister and I in sleeping bags in our friend's
backyard, giggled ourselves to sleep while
our father watched our house burn, the flames
mingling with the constellations, the only stars
that fell were the tears clinging to my father's lashes,
colliding and reforming as black holes, a gravitational
pull so strong not even light can escape.

Now in the summer of backyard stars I see our collapse
in slow motion: the brown of my skin fading, the shine
of us dimming, a star dying and collapsing and collapsing
and sinking into the center of the galaxy and becoming
a black hole.

REMEMBER THE OCEAN

A literal ocean rushes beneath our skin. Every morning the tide surges in me, reminding me that even though we no longer speak, even though my toes are no longer buried in the sand, the salt air that once filled my nostrils is still inside me, the ocean in me will always remember the ocean in you.

POSTCARDS NEVER WRITTEN

I saw the sunset today and remembered
the times we watched it together.

I ~~don't~~ miss you, ~~but~~ I wonder
if you miss me.

I think you fell in love with
all the poems about you.

I sleep better at night without you.

(left blank, only your name and address, written
in block letters)

STARVED

Do not mistake my silence
for absence: every day I think
of you and every day I say
nothing—no message sent,
no phone call made, no
letter mailed. With you it had
to be—has to be—all or none.
I loved you once, I think
you kept part of my heart
tucked into a pocket,
held close to the warmth
of your body. Even though
we no longer speak, look
between the silences, find
the quiet meaning in the spaces
between the words, small enough
to swallow whole. Language
is a kind of hunger and I am
always starved.

PARIS IMPLODING

In the postcard the children sit perched
on the ledge of an unbroken sidewalk
in Paris. Her hands clasped in her lap,
his hand angled toward her. They
are seven or maybe eight and flirting—
innocent as bees drunk on pollen, bumbling
and gentle. They have no way of knowing
their nights will soon be filled with the shriek
of air raid sirens, that bombs will sing
through the air, an unending dirge.
When I was in Paris I didn't
look for the strike marks of bombs.
Instead I bought expensive lingerie
and ate chocolate crepes and ignored
my imploding marriage. The trip
was my idea, the city I'd lusted for
since I was a teenager. My husband,
indifferent to travel and French wine,
tolerated everything but me. We
separated two weeks after we
returned, the suitcases pulled again
from the attic and filled with his
things. I taped the postcard to my
bathroom mirror, a reminder
of a time before the destruction.

I'M ALWAYS THE REFRAIN IN YOUR SONGS

>*Please don't keep me.*
>   *(Please don't leave me.)*
>   —William Fitzsimmons, "After All"

You promised and pledged and slipped
a ring onto my manicured finger and we

kissed as petals fluttered down around
us, soft as butterfly wings. Now your hand

is on the doorknob and my heart is beneath
your feet and I know this moment will become

a song—your soft tenor and the callouses
on your fingers strumming the chords

of our discord. Another woman will fall
for your smooth voice and your rough hands

and later, you'll write happy songs about her
but I'll always be there—the quiet harmony

that builds every song, that built your heart
into something another woman would hold.

STARFISH

They held it high above their heads,
hoisted their prickly trophy up,
mouths open in triumph.
It was bigger than my hand,
bigger than your hand,
big as a giant's hand.

Throw it back! I yelled,
squinted into the salty air,
felt the humidity curl my hair
as I shaded my eyes from the
brightness that bounced off the sea.

They tossed it away,
mad they'd shown me,
mad I'd made them leave it.

You swam out after the kids left,
drug it to shore.
I traced my water-puckered fingers
over its rough surface,
amazed it was a living creature.

I'm going to keep it, you said.
I argued but you wouldn't listen,
you wanted this treasure from the sea,
a permanent reminder of the months
we spent arguing in the salty air.

You soaked it in bleach,
killing it and weakening its
once-hard structure.
It crumbled in your hands when
you pulled it out.

I looked away.

BLOOD ORANGE

My first marriage tasted like blood
orange—that first bite tart
on my tongue, slowly melting
to sweet near the back of my teeth.
The bright orange peel hiding
the crimson flesh inside—like you hid
your raging jealousy behind your
bright smile, kept it contained
till I loved that bloody
fruit too much to know how to live
without it. Eventually the taste dulled,
left an aftertaste in my mouth
I could finally escape. Eventually
the season ended, the fruit impossible
to find, your jealousy impossible
to ignore. I went to an orchard,
picked every variety of fruit
I could find, left the blood orange
trees untouched, never dug
my fingers into the thick rind again,
never had the sticky juices run
down my hands again, never swallowed
your bitter jealousy with a slice
of crimson fruit again.

SURRENDER

During the short summer months we hung
our laundry on the clothesline, linen
flapping in the wind, announcing surrender.
The only battles I knew were the ones I raged
with my sister, fighting imaginary foes
and sometimes each other. We dutifully hung
the bras and underwear on the inside lines,
sheltered from view by the towels and t-shirts,
just as our mother taught us. The clothes smelled
like summer sun but were always stiff, no matter
the fabric softener my mother added to the wash.

When I followed a man I loved to Puerto Rico,
played house on that island, we had no dryer
so once again I strung clothes along a line
that stretched across our balcony. Every
afternoon a thunderstorm rolled through
and every day I made a choice: mad dash
to collect the nearly dry clothes or let them
get soaked and dry again. Eventually I left
the island, his jealousy a battle I could no longer
fight. I left the linens drying on the line,
waving in surrender or goodbye.

GOAT OF MY HEART

Goats will eat anything, their teeth and stomachs able
to chew through whatever they consume. In DC, the city
employs goats to eat through the wild poison ivy that grows
uncontrolled in Congressional Cemetery, the goats wandering
among the headstones, caring for them in an efficient way
that must be some sort of love. My heart is a goat, gnawing
through everything—him: a tin can that cuts my mouth
and throat as I swallow, the sharp taste of blood filling
my mouth, my belly full but with nothing to nourish me.
And then the other him: the dew-licked grass, tender and filling.
My heart always eats this last, unable to understand
the one who is good for me.

PEARL

I hold memories like sand
on my tongue—the heat
of your hands on my skin,
the sound of my name
on your lips. I roll these around,
bite them with my teeth, wonder
if I should swallow the memory
of you, let it fester from within
or if I should keep mouthing
your memory until a pale pearl
emerges, until I can wear it like
a talisman at the base of my throat.

SELF-PORTRAIT AS A FORM REJECTION LETTER

We appreciate[1] the opportunity
to read[2] your work, we know
there are many journals to choose[3]
from and we're honored you chose
ours. Unfortunately[4] your poems
weren't for us and we'll have to pass.
Do not take this as a reflection[5]
on the caliber of your work. We wish[6]
you the best of luck[7] placing
these poems elsewhere.[8]

Sincerely,
the editors

1. The word appreciate means "to recognize the full worth of" and you wonder, has anyone fully appreciated you? Remember when you made him dinner, how you carefully cooked the chicken to ensure it wasn't dried out and opened the wine to breathe and only had one glass before he arrived. And how he didn't notice the way you'd folded the napkins or that the music playing was your favorite artist. How he wished for beer instead of wine. How he fucked you on the table after but didn't help with the dishes.
2. Oh how you read—every book of poems, every novel. You eat up stories. Even when they don't end happily ever after they still seem better than your life.
3. So many choices: stay or leave? Go to bed annoyed again or tackle the beast you've been battling. Acknowledge things aren't okay or just turn out the lights, close your eyes, sleep.

4. It seems so simple to say: unfortunately things aren't working out. Yet you never can, these words remain lodged in your throat. You learn to speak around them.
5. Of course this will reflect poorly on you—another failed relationship, another failed attempt at life, another failure to stack on top of the last.
6. You were never one to make wishes. When given a coin to throw into the fountain you pocketed it instead. A falling star made you cry. Blowing out the birthday candles never seemed worthy of a wish. Now you wonder if you've squandered all those wishes, all those chances to ask for something better.
7. You don't believe in luck, despite that four-leaf clover tattooed to your belly. You were nineteen, you can't be held accountable for such foolishness.
8. You begin wishing you could be somewhere else. Wishing, like Dorothy, you could click your heels together and magically be returned to a happier place. You buy red shoes. You wear them when you finally get the courage to leave.

HOW TO RUN

Lace up your shoes, put one foot
in front of the other. Repeat until
his name is no longer circling
in your mind, until all you hear
and think and breathe is your footfall,
gentle against the pavement.
Invest in good shoes, sweat-wicking
clothes, and a quality sports bra: trust
me, it's worth the cost. When it's raining,
wear a visor to keep your vision clear—
you'll still need to log your miles. If you
don't, you'll curl up on the couch, phone
in your hand, scrolling through pictures
of him. You'll want to call him so run
an extra mile instead, run until you're soaked
through, shoes sloshing with every
step, but you're no longer tempted
to hear his voice. Wake with the sunrise,
watch the sky lighten as you crest
a hill, your gait easier than it's been
in weeks. Run faster, push your pace
until your legs quake and every atom
aches from something that isn't his touch.
Sleep hard every night, your body wonderfully
exhausted. Dream of the hills you will tackle
the next morning. Wake rested and ready,
your body craving movement, your mind

clear and unencumbered by any thoughts other than today's route. Lace up your shoes, put one foot in front of the other. Repeat.

EXQUISITE BLOODY, BEATING HEART

CONSTELLATION

He pulls it out of his pocket, bright
and eager, extends his hand and drops
it into my open palm. A delicate
necklace with five tiny stars strung across
the chain. My smile outshines the galaxy,
You've given me my own constellation, I say,
stringing it around my neck, the gold stars falling
across my collar bones. He reaches out, lightly
fingering the stars. He closes his eyes,
makes a wish.

THE WEIGHT OF WATER

You pull me down, your love
the weight of water, capable

of both drowning and quenching
thirst. This is a time of treading

water, I am fighting
to keep us above the waves,

our relationship slipping, the weight
sinking through my wet fingers.

I pull in long strokes, I learned
to swim as a child, summer

lessons at the local pool.
I dip my head beneath the blue

then turn and breathe the clear
air as I surface. I drag us

to the shore, lie back on the grainy sand.
Catch my breath before wading back in.

POMPEII

We skipped the guided tour and spent
the day wandering the ruins,
eventually finding the famous
figures, forever captured curled
in sleep or in terror as ashes rained
down. I can't imagine
what it was like, an eruption
so powerful an entire city was buried.
Until I spent the day wandering it,
until I learned only ⅔ of the city
has been unearthed, I thought
it was merely a small village, not
a bustling mecca of 20,000.
We found our way to the back,
where civilization still lay buried.
We wove our way to a deserted
spot, then fucked against a wall—
so young and alive
in that dead city.

I DON'T WRITE MANY NICE POEMS ABOUT HIM

I remember mornings we drove
to the beach, windows rolled down,
my long hair a cape flying
wild. We always stopped
at the bodega near the house, always
ordered the same thing—four coffees
with milk and sugar and a loaf of French
bread. We sipped coffee while driving, tore
off chunks of the warm bread. By the time
we reached the beach, half the bread
and coffee was gone. We kicked off
our shoes, dug our toes into the still
cool sand and ate the rest as the sun rose.
The day spent in the warm sun; salt water
curling my hair and leaving a thin crust
on my skin. I wrap my hands around
my warm mug, my kitchen hundreds
of miles from the island we called
home. I can almost feel the breeze on my skin.
I don't think of the rest—how jealousy tore
at us, how his control broke me
little by little. I drink my coffee and pull
out the ingredients to bake bread.

JOLENE

> *And I could easily understand how you could take my man but you don't know what he means to me.*
> —Dolly Parton, "Jolene"

We were over by then, completely
finished. We'd both been through
the five stages of grief but I
circled back to depression.

You asked what you could do
and I said, *Come over. Hold me.*
We lay in bed that night, the first
time in months and you held
me while I cried then said,
Please don't write about this.
I don't want Jolene to know.

I'd been the one to cause
the end, I know that, but you
moved on so fast—as if
the seven years we spent together
were best remembered through
the lens of a new love.

You stayed the night, holding
me, breathing softly
beside me. You left
before dawn.

I waited eight years
to write this poem.

I hope she
understands.

TO MY EX WHO ASKED IF EVERY POEM WAS ABOUT HIM

I wish you happiness, but the kind that makes you think of me after your wife has fallen asleep. I wish you 2% raises and average performance evals. I wish you casseroles and Bud Light. I wish you vacations to Disney World in July. I wish you khakis and plaid button-ups. I wish you sex but only missionary position and only with the lights out. I wish you calendar reminders and capped teeth. I wish you individually wrapped low-fat cheese slices and turkey bacon which insults two animals. I wish you mayonnaise and store-bought white bread. I wish you decaf coffee. I wish you "sleeping in" till 7am on Sundays. I wish you instant oatmeal microwaved each morning for your heart health. I wish you a tie each Father's Day and a birthday card received a week late. I wish you a daughter who writes poetry filled with metaphors about a complicated family relationship. I wish you a football team that never makes the playoffs and a son who's an average soccer player. I wish you this poem popping up first the next time you Google me.

POEM IN WHICH NOTHING BAD EVER HAPPENS TO ME

I catch the train.
I make the flight.
I get the promotion.

I never worry
if my waist is small enough, the number
on the scale never dips
to double digits, I don't cling
to my own hip bones like a steering wheel
of an out-of-control car. I don't eat
an apple and two rice cakes
for lunch for an entire year.
Instead I plant an orchard, I grow
six varieties of apples and I bake warm
cinnamon-scented pies. I eat them
with my hands, fingers digging
into the warm filling.

I never take him back after the first time
or the second or the third. We never
even date, he remains the friend
of a friend I met over dinner.

I don't have an affair, my married
coworker doesn't push me
up against the conference wall
and kiss me, fingers lifting the hem
of my skirt so he can slide inside me

after our Monday staff meeting.
My husband doesn't read
my emails, my journal. He doesn't
throw the lamp, it doesn't smash,
my fingertips don't bleed from the pale
gray shards. I don't receive threats,
I don't have to take out a restraining
order, I don't cry
in front of the cops, my mother doesn't
say *but he was always so nice to us* . . .

I don't have a fight with my mother
on Thanksgiving, she doesn't call
me a terrible daughter before hanging up,
she doesn't bite back the words *ungrateful
bitch* because they never enter her mind.
We don't spend the next two years
in silence.

My dad doesn't get sick, he doesn't spend
the last 30 years of his life in a revolving
door of doctors and drugs and hospital stays.

My sister doesn't get diagnosed
with the same disease that chased
my father to his grave.

My dog doesn't age. Her face doesn't
turn white, she doesn't slow—instead
she chases bunnies and squirrels

with continued vigor and gets
into bathroom trashes and eats
anything she finds on the ground.

I miss the train.
I miss the flight.
I don't get the promotion.

THE FIRST POST-MARRIAGE FUCK

You'll meet him in a bar, happy
hour. You're with a friend and he's alone,
new in town. You will misuse the word *brooding*
when you describe him. You will get his number
that night but will not take him home.
He will tell you about his girlfriend
in Hong Kong, how they're free
to see other people in the year
they're apart. You won't believe him
but you won't challenge him either.
He'll come over two days after
Thanksgiving, complaining of the bad
haircut he got. You will laugh,
run your fingers through his butchered hair,
kiss him, fuck him. It will be delicious sex.
You will settle into a sex and Sunday
football routine. You don't care
about football but you like fucking him.
You will make plans to spend
New Year's eve together—
a club in DC, a 90s band. A week before
Christmas you'll be thumbing through
the cards on his mantle and you'll read
the words
    fiancé, my fiancé.
That night, after you've fucked him
you'll ask what his fiancé's name is.
He'll notice

the word *fiancé* and he will pause
before answering:
    Fiona.
You'll continue seeing him
    fucking him
until New Year's Eve.
Just before midnight
you'll be separated and you'll kiss
the man you're dancing with,
the man you'll eventually date—
he won't have a girlfriend or fiancé
and while it won't last
it will be honest.
You'll go home with Fiona's fiancé
that night and fuck him.
The next morning you'll tell
him to fuck off.

THE CRAIGSLIST MISSED CONNECTION
I DIDN'T WRITE

You boarded the green line at the Navy
Yard metro stop, green Chucks paired
with the DC uniform: khakis,
a button-up, tie loose at your neck.
You wore Clark Kent glasses & a tribal
swirl peeked out from under your
rolled-up sleeves. I wore a black
dress, flip-flops replacing the day's
heels, my hair long & dark, my nails
short & red. You caught me
staring, eyeing the edges
of your mouth. I didn't look
away. The train pulled
into L'Enfant station & bodies
streamed out. You exited, I followed,
crossed the tracks to the other side, boarded
the yellow line toward Huntington. Half a car
between us as we eye-fucked each other—
neither brave enough
to approach in the sudden brilliance
of the afternoon as the train pushed
above ground. Two stops later I exited, looked
back at you one last time. You stared & I lifted
my hand, fluttered my fingers
goodbye, the sun reflecting
on my ring.

BEFORE THE OCCASION OF YOUR DEATH

The scent of your deodorant mixed with the steam
from the shower. How you build a fire, getting it to catch

the first time. The lasagna you make, that requires
three hours of simmering on the stove, perfuming

the house with a rich tomato smell. How you fold
your t-shirts with precision but hate making the bed.

Your love of children's cereal, the more rainbow
colors the better. Your big hands and small feet.

That at forty-one you still don't have any gray hair.
How you read to me that night in the ER, when

it took four hours to be seen and I whimpered
in pain. How you laugh because I can't cut

a pizza evenly. Your delight when I bought you
a five-pound gummy bear and you sliced it

like prime rib, starting with an ear. How you call
cauliflower *ghost broccoli* and refuse to eat it.

How you recreated your Oma's cucumber salad
through trial and error because she died before

she could tell you the recipe. The way you dance
with me at weddings even though you dance

like a cliché. How this list is incomplete,
how it can never be complete, how you're still

breathing and living but I know one day you won't.

HONEST ANSWER

He asks me if I'm happy and I answer *yes* without
even thinking. The honest answer is *mostly* because

I'm not sure I could ever be completely happy. I wonder
if I'm broken, a talking doll that only speaks

one phrase when you pull the string on her back.
The next morning I wake early, my husband heavy

with sleep beside me. I ease out of bed, stand in my cold
kitchen while my coffee brews. By the time I finish

my cup the sky is on fire with sunrise. I think
of dressing quickly and slipping out for a run so I can witness

the world waking. Instead I strip off my clothes and slide
back into bed, wake my husband with my body, try to rewrite

the word *yes* into an honest answer.

THE PLEASURE OF HATING

I hate alarm clocks on Monday
mornings—the end of the weekend

heralded by the blaring
at 5am. I hate country music,

the sadness and twang and subtle
racism I hear in every song. I hate

the trucks that scare my dog, turn
her into 50 pounds of cower and fear.

I hate loud bars and indifferent
bartenders. I hate coconut, health

benefits aside, it makes me want
to vomit. I hate Christmas, the forced

cheer, the pressure of spending
the day with the mother who refuses

to speak to me the rest of the year.
I hate Mother's Day and Father's

Day but for different reasons—one
because there's nothing to celebrate,

the other because he's dying.
I delight in detesting all of these

things. And love loving
you so much after that.

GARDEN

I'd forgotten how lucky I am to have you. It's so easy
to focus on life's daily annoyances—you never

vacuum unless I ask, your eyes blind
to the dirt ringing the carpet—that I forget your love

is a garden I must tend. My farmer-father plants
an acre-large garden; since retiring he doesn't know

what to do with his free time so he does
what he's always done: makes magic

with his hands, the black soil growing
8-foot tall sunflowers and more cucumbers

than my mother can pickle. This year I planted
my first garden—rosemary, basil, tomatoes,

peppers, and cucumbers—the dirt contained
in boxes along the fence. I was ecstatic

with the offerings from my tiny plot; you made
your Oma's cucumber salad, the one she never

wrote down but you somehow replicated.
I diced tomatoes, plucked basil leaves, offered

it up to you on a plate. *Here, eat my love.*

ELEGY FOR MY STILL-LIVING HUSBAND

We joke about who will die
first but we both know it will
likely be you. We hold hands
while walking the dog, make
her "talk" and argue
about who she loves more.
I adopted her years ago
but before long we both craved
your scent. One day I'll donate
your organs and hope
your eyes, your lungs, your heart
live on in another. For now, I put
my feet on your calves in bed
and you yelp at the cold then
move your legs to sandwich
my frozen toes and curl your
whole body around me, reminding
me of the home I found in you.

LOVE IS A LESION ON YOUR BRAIN

When the headaches started again
you offered ibuprofen and understanding
and drawn shades. When a train wreck
woke me in the middle of the night, you broke
out the Valium and Percocet and told me not to
cry because that makes it worse, then held me
till I fell into an ocean of quiet. Prescription bottles
line the bathroom sink like dominoes, knock one down
and watch me fall deeper. When the neurologist said,
we found something, you held my hand, a portrait of calm
in the fury of the storm building in my brain.
When the neurosurgeon photographed every slice
and angle of the lesion I would eventually name
Napoleon, you offered to shave your head.
I walk in the door and you know if it's a night
for wine or for quiet darkness—you've learned
to read the foreign tongue of my grimaces, my sighs.
I've been a pincushion, needles placed into my skin
as delicately as a wreath placed upon a grave.
I've removed red wine, peanut butter, loud noises,
MSG, chocolate, bright lights, and coffee from my diet.
I've been on so many different drugs
the pharmacists greet me by name.
I'm sorry our nights have become cluttered
with medicine that makes me so dizzy I trace the walls
to keep from falling, that make me unable to sleep
and escape this madness, that make me cringe
when you speak above a whisper.

I hope you know when I'm closed up
in our dark bedroom I'm praying to God
and Buddha and Allah and Darwin
that this ends soon. I'm scared you'll buy flowers
for some other girl who doesn't live
in the gutted carcass of herself.
I'm worried you'll decide that the idea
of *in sickness and in health* is too much for you.
Baby, my head hasn't stopped screaming for six months
but at least it's screaming *I fucking love you.*

EVENTUALLY EVOLUTION

Remember we didn't start like this—we didn't always
have these (mostly) hairless bodies, didn't walk upright,
didn't love with such ferocity—these things took millennia
to develop. From amoeba to boneless invertebrate—
jellyfish or mollusk—to fish with legs that eventually
pushed itself up onto land and walked, through pure
effort and a million years of slowly evolving. Eventually
it got bigger, grew fur, pushed past monkeys into some
early Neanderthal version of a human—not very smart
and quite ugly. Eventually we figured out fire
and the wheel and hand tools and the Earth kept
circling the sun and the land broke apart and drifted
into the continents we more or less have today. Humans
started wearing pants and we went to the moon
and we dropped LSD and bombs on other countries
and eventually I met you and the muscle in my chest,
which took millennia to evolve into this exquisite bloody,
beating heart found you and I knew, this is exactly
what we'd been aiming for from the very beginning.

THANKS

Thank you to my husband, Jay, for always supporting my poetry endeavors, even when I say I'm going to start an independent poetry press that probably won't make any money. Your logical, scientist brain may not appreciate poetry, but I know your heart sees mine. Thank you for being my person and for evolving with me.

Thank you to my critique group, for often being the first eyes to see these poems and giving me honest and valuable feedback—Queenies forever! Special thanks to Chelsea for being a beta reader for the entire manuscript.

Thank you to Sita and Whitney—for each and every motherfucking pep talk.

Thank you to Heather—our weekly hikes and talks keep me grounded and sane.

Thank you to Shuly, Shaindel, and Kelly for writing such kind things about my collection.

Finally, thank you reader—for believing in poetry, for supporting poets and independent presses, and for reading these words. I hope you find something to love in here.

ACKNOWLEDGMENTS & NOTES

The poet kindly thanks the following journals which first gave her poems a home, sometimes in earlier forms:

Vending Machine Press: Autobiography of Eve
Dirty Paws Poetry: We Carry
Thank You for Swallowing: Alternative Names for Woman, Promotion
Rogue Agent: We're Told to Smile
Selcouth Station: Her Becoming, Post-Sex Snack
Rising Phoenix Press: To The Man Who Shouted "What does your pussy taste like?!" as I Ran By
Anti-Heroin Chic: Gasoline
Moonchild Magazine: My Current Favorite Is Called Blackmail
Germ Magazine: First Date, Starfish, Love Is a Lesion on Your Brain
Writers Resist: Poem Where I Mix-Up Fairy Tales
Whatever Keeps the Lights on—Stolen Time Anthology: On the Way to a Cocktail Reception for Work
Glass: A Journal of Poetry: How Empty Those Roads Were, This Body
Mookychick: Tradition (originally published as Fables & Fairy Tales)
Cephalopress: First Punch, Love Poem to My Scoliosis
Kissing Dynamite: Butcher, I'm Always the Refrain in Your Songs
Bloodsugar Poetry: A Girl Becomes a Woman
Magnolia Review: Original Sin, A Choose Your Own Path Poem

Burning House Press: Other Than Desire
Slant: Hunger Lectures Me
Riggwelter: Skinny Dreams
Dovecote Magazine: Did Not
Mojave Heart Journal: Sixteen, Pompeii
Where is the River: Construction, Imagine What My Body Will Sound Like, Morning Tableau
Misfit Magazine: Ode to My Vibrator
Rhythm & Bones: Collapse
goodbaad poetry journal: Starved
Animal Heart Press: Remember the Ocean, Postcards Never Written, Constellation
Crepe & Penn: Paris Imploding
Linden Avenue: Blood Orange
QA Poetry: Surrender
Okay Donkey: Goat of My Heart
Gemstone Piano: Pearl
Dodging the Rain: Self-Portrait as a Form Rejection Letter
perhappened: How to Run
Firefly Magazine: The Weight of Water
Thin Air Magazine: I Don't Write Many Nice Poems About Him
Feminine Collective: Jolene
Cabinet of Heed: To My Ex Who Asked if Every Poem Was About Him
Halfway Down the Stairs: Poem in Which Nothing Bad Ever Happens to Me
Quail Bell Magazine: The First Post-Marriage Fuck
District Lines: The Craigslist Missed Connection I Didn't Write
Orange Blossom Review: Before the Occasion of Your Death

Cardiff Review: Garden
Merak Magazine: Elegy for My Still-Living Husband
Feral: Eventually Evolution

"Autobiography of Eve" borrows the first line and its title from Ansel Elkins's poem with the same title.

"Her Becoming" borrows lines from *sometimes i wish i felt the side effects* by Danez Smith.

"To My Ex Who Asked if Every Poem I Wrote Was About Him" was inspired by "Dry Cake Wishes and Tap Water Dreams" by Rachel Wiley.

"Poem in Which Nothing Bad Ever Happens to Me" was inspired by a poem by Jameson Fitzpatrick with the same title.

"The Pleasure of Hating" borrows its title and last line from Laure-Anne Bosselar's poem with the same title.

Orange Blossom Review nominated "Before the Occasion of Your Death" for a Best of the Net.

ABOUT THE AUTHOR

Courtney LeBlanc is the author of the full-length collections *Exquisite Bloody, Beating Heart* (Riot in Your Throat) and *Beautiful & Full of Monsters* (Vegetarian Alcoholic Press). She is also the founder and Editor-in-Chief of Riot in Your Throat, an independent poetry press. She loves nail polish, tattoos, and a soy latte each morning. Follow her on twitter: @wordperv, and IG: @wordperv79.

ABOUT THE PRESS

Riot in Your Throat is an independent press that publishes fierce, feminist poetry.

Support independent authors, artists, and presses.

Visit us online:
www.riotinyourthroat.com

www.ingramcontent.com/pod-product-compliance
Lightning Source LLC
Chambersburg PA
CBHW031234260625
28691CB00004BA/112